Atlantis Books

Words of Wisdom from Ancient Greece

Words
of Wisdom
from Ancient Greece

Translated by
Alexander Zaphiriou

Illustrated by
Panagiotis Stavropoulos

AIORA

Cover design by Panagiotis Stavropoulos
Ink on recycled paper produced by Kyra Stratoudaki

ISBN: 978-618-5048-71-6

AIORA PRESS
11 Mavromichali st.
Athens 10679 - Greece
tel: +30 210 3839000
www.aiora.gr

ΧΡΗΣΙΜΑ ΕΙΔΩΣ

ΟΥΧ Ο ΠΟΛΛΑ ΕΙΔΩΣ

ΣΟΦΟΣ

It is knowing worthwhile things,
rather than lots of things,
that makes one wise.

AESCHYLUS
(525–456 BCE, tragedian)

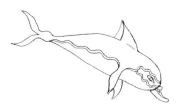

Η ΙΣΧΥΣ
ΕΝ ΤΗ ΕΝΩΣΕΙ

Strength is in unity.

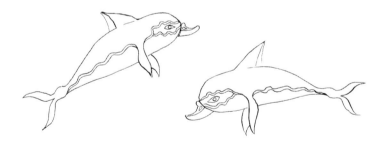

AESOP
(620–560 BCE, fabulist)

ΣΤΟΥΣ ΓΟΝΕΙΣ
ΟΦΕΙΛΟΜΕΝ ΤΟ ΖΗΝ
ΣΤΟΥΣ ΔΕ ΔΙΔΑΣΚΑΛΟΥΣ
ΤΟ ΕΥ ΖΗΝ

We owe our being to our parents
and our wellbeing to our teachers.

ALEXANDER THE GREAT
(356–323 BCE, King of Macedonia)

ΛΕΩΝ ΜΕΝ ΟΝΥΞΙ ΚΡΑΤΕΙ

ΚΕΡΑΣΙ ΔΕ ΒΟΥΣ

ΑΝΘΡΩΠΟΣ ΔΕ ΝΩ

A lion prevails by its claws,
a bull by its horns,
and a man by his brains.

ANAXAGORAS
(c. 500–427 BCE, philosopher and astronomer)

ΠΡΟΣΕΧΕΙΝ ΤΟΙΣ ΕΧΘΡΟΙΣ
ΠΡΩΤΟΙ ΓΑΡ ΤΩΝ ΑΜΑΡΤΗΜΑΤΩΝ
ΑΙΣΘΑΝΟΝΤΑΙ

Heed your enemies;
they are the first
to mark your errors.

ANTISTHENES

(445–360 BCE, Cynic philosopher)

ΟΥΚ ΕΝ ΤΩ ΠΟΛΛΩ ΤΟ ΕΥ

ΑΛΛΑ ΕΝ ΤΩ ΕΥ ΤΟ ΠΟΛΥ

Goodness lies not in abundance:
abundance lies in goodness.

ARISTOTLE
(384–322 BCE, philosopher)

Η ΦΥΣΙΣ ΜΗΔΕΝ
ΜΗΤΕ ΑΤΕΛΕΣ ΠΟΙΕΙ
ΜΗΤΕ ΜΑΤΗΝ

Nothing nature makes
is imperfect or in vain.

ARISTOTLE
(384–322 BCE, philosopher)

ΠΑΣΑΝ ΓΛΩΣΣΑ ΒΑΣΑΝΙΣΕ

Ponder well
what you say.

ARISTOPHANES
(445–386 BCE, comedian)

ΑΡΧΗ ΑΝΔΡΑ ΔΕΙΚΝΥΣΙ

Power reveals the man.

BIAS OF PRIENE
(625–540 BCE, one of the Seven Sages)

ΤΟΠΩΝ ΜΕΤΑΒΟΛΑΙ

ΟΥΤΕ ΦΡΟΝΗΣΙΝ ΔΙΔΑΣΚΟΥΣΙΝ

ΟΥΤΕ ΑΦΡΟΣΥΝΗΝ ΑΦΑΙΡΟΥΝΤΑΙ

A change of place
neither teaches probity
nor removes foolishness.

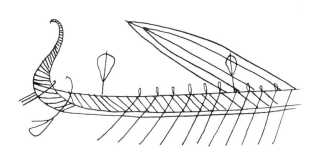

BIAS OF PRIENE
(625–540 BCE, one of the Seven Sages)

ΓΝΩΘΙ ΣΑΥΤΟΝ

ΧΡΟΝΟΥ ΦΕΙΔΟΥ

ΣΠΕΥΔΕ ΒΡΑΔΕΩΣ

Know yourself.

Be sparing with time.

Hasten slowly.

CHILON OF SPARTA
(6th c. BCE, one of the Seven Sages)

ΜΕΤΡΟΝ ΑΡΙΣΤΟΝ

Moderation is best.

CLEOBULUS OF LINDOS
(6th c. BCE, one of the Seven Sages)

ΕΥΠΟΙΙΑΣ ΗΣ ΕΤΥΧΕΣ

ΜΝΗΜΟΝΕΥΕ

Be mindful of the benefactions
you have been granted.

CLEOBULUS OF LINDOS
(6th c. BCE, one of the Seven Sages)

ΤΟ ΝΙΚΑΝ ΕΑΥΤΟΝ

ΠΑΣΩΝ ΝΙΚΩΝ ΠΡΩΤΗ ΚΑΙ ΑΡΙΣΤΗ

ΤΟ ΔΕ ΗΤΤΑΣΘΑΙ ΑΥΤΟΝ ΥΦ ΕΑΥΤΟΥ

ΑΙΣΧΙΣΤΟΝ ΚΑΙ ΚΑΚΙΣΤΟΝ

Vanquishing oneself
is the first and finest of victories;
being vanquished by oneself
is the vilest and
most ignoble thing.

DEMOCRITUS
(470–370 BCE, philosopher)

ΠΟΘΗΤΟΣ ΕΙΝΑΙ ΜΑΛΛΟΝ

Η ΦΟΒΕΡΟΣ

ΚΑΤΑ ΒΙΟΝ ΠΡΟΑΙΡΟΥ

ΟΝ ΠΑΝΤΕΣ ΦΟΒΟΥΝΤΑΙ

ΠΑΝΤΑΣ ΦΟΒΕΙΤΑΙ

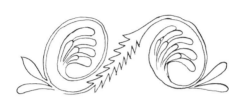

Be loved rather
than feared.
He whom everyone fears,
fears everyone.

DEMOCRITUS
(470–370 BCE, philosopher)

ΒΙΟΣ ΑΝΕΟΡΤΑΣΤΟΣ

ΜΑΚΡΑ ΟΔΟΣ

ΑΠΑΝΔΟΧΕΥΤΟΣ

Life without festivity
is a long journey without refuge.

DEMOCRITUS
(470–370 BCE, philosopher)

ΑΝΘΡΩΠΟΙΣ ΠΑΣΙ

ΤΑΥΤΟ ΑΓΑΘΟΝ ΚΑΙ ΑΛΗΘΕΣ

ΗΔΥ ΔΕ ΑΛΛΩ ΑΛΛΟ

The good and the true
are the same for everyone.
What is pleasurable differs
from one to another.

DEMOCRITUS
(470–370 BCE, philosopher)

ΧΑΛΕΠΩΤΕΡΟΝ ΤΟ ΦΥΛΑΤΤΕΙΝ

ΤΟΥ ΚΤΗΣΑΣΘΑΙ

It's harder to keep
than to acquire.

DEMOSTHENES
(384–322 BCE, Athenian orator)

ΠΑΙΔΕΙΑ
ΤΟΙΣ ΜΕΝ ΝΕΟΙΣ ΣΩΦΡΟΣΥΝΗ
ΤΟΙΣ ΔΕ ΠΕΝΗΣΙ ΠΛΟΥΤΟΣ
ΤΟΙΣ ΔΕ ΠΛΟΥΣΙΟΙΣ ΚΟΣΜΟΣ

Education
is farsightedness for the young,
wealth for the poor,
enhancement for the rich.

DIOGENES
(410–323 BCE, Cynic philosopher)

ΜΕΛΕΤΑΝ ΟΥΝ ΧΡΗ
ΤΑ ΠΟΙΟΥΝΤΑ ΤΗΝ ΕΥΔΑΙΜΟΝΙΑΝ
ΕΙΠΕΡ ΠΑΡΟΥΣΗΣ ΜΕΝ ΑΥΤΗΣ
ΠΑΝΤΑ ΕΧΟΜΕΝ
ΑΠΟΥΣΗΣ ΔΕ
ΠΑΝΤΑ ΠΡΑΤΤΟΜΕΝ
ΕΙΣ ΤΟ ΤΑΥΤΗΝ ΕΧΕΙΝ

We must ponder
on what brings happiness,
for in having it
we have everything,
but if it's missing
we would do anything
to gain it.

Epicurus
(341–270 BCE, philosopher)

TAPATTEI TOYΣ ANΘPΩΠOYΣ

OY TA ΠPAΓMATA

AΛΛA TA ΠEPI TΩN ΠPAΓMATΩN

ΔOΓMATA

People are perturbed
not by the things
that happen
but by their views
on that
which happens.

EPICTETUS
(50–120 CE, Stoic philosopher)

ΤΙΣ ΕΙΝΑΙ ΘΕΛΕΙΣ ΣΑΥΤΩ

ΠΡΩΤΟΝ ΕΙΠΕ

ΕΙΘΕ ΟΥΤΩΣ ΠΟΙΕΙ

Α ΠΟΙΕΙΣ

Say first who you wish to be
and then, whatever you do,
do accordingly.

EPICTETUS
(50–120 CE, Stoic philosopher)

ΡΩΜΗ ΑΜΑΘΗΣ

ΠΟΛΛΑΚΙΣ ΤΙΚΤΕΙ ΒΛΑΒΗΝ

Untutored strength
often begets harm.

EURIPIDES
(480–406 BCE, tragedian)

ΤΑ ΠΑΝΤΑ ΡΕΙ

ΚΑΙ ΟΥΔΕΝ ΜΕΝΕΙ

Everything flows
and nothing abides.

HERACLITUS
(544–484 BCE, Ionian philosopher)

ΕΑΝ ΜΗ ΕΛΠΗΤΑΙ

ΑΝΕΛΠΙΣΤΟΝ

ΟΥΚ ΕΞΕΥΡΗΣΕΙ

If you do not hope
for what is unhoped-for,
you'll never find it.

HERACLITUS
(544–484 BCE, Ionian philosopher)

ΟΥΚ ΑΕΙ ΘΕΡΟΣ ΕΣΣΕΤΑΙ

ΠΟΙΕΙΣΘΕ ΚΑΛΙΑΣ

It won't be summer always;
reap while you can.

HESIOD
(7th c. BCE, poet)

ΚΑΛΛΙΟΝ
ΤΟ ΠΡΟΛΑΜΒΑΝΕΙΝ
Η ΤΟ ΘΕΡΑΠΕΥΕΙΝ

Prevention is better
than cure.

HIPPOCRATES
(460–377 BCE, physician)

ΟΠΠΟΙΟΝ ΚΙ ΕΙΠΗΣΘΑ ΕΠΟΣ

ΤΟΙΟΝ ΚΙ ΕΠΑΚΟΥΣΑΙΣ

The words you speak are the ones
you will hear spoken to you.

HOMER
(c. 800–750 BCE, poet)

ΦΡΟΝΗΣΗΣ ΜΕΝ ΜΗΔΕΠΟΤΕ

ΕΠΙ ΣΕΑΥΤΩ ΜΕΓΑ

ΑΛΛΑ ΜΗΔΕ ΚΑΤΑΦΡΟΝΗΣΗΣ

ΣΕΑΥΤΟΥ

Neither imagine
yourself superior,
nor be contemptuous
of yourself.

ISOCRATES
(436–338 BCE, Athenian orator)

ΜΗΔΕΝΙ ΣΥΜΦΟΡΑΝ ΟΝΕΙΔΙΣΗΣ

ΚΟΙΝΗ ΓΑΡ Η ΤΥΧΗ

ΚΑΙ ΤΟ ΜΕΛΛΟΝ ΑΟΡΑΤΟΝ

Do not scoff at anyone's disaster.
Fortune's vicissitudes happen to all
and the future is unknown.

ISOCRATES
(436–338 BCE, Athenian orator)

ΤΟ ΔΙΣ ΕΞΑΜΑΡΤΕΙΝ ΤΟ ΑΥΤΟΝ

ΟΥΚ ΑΝΔΡΟΣ ΣΟΦΟΥ

It is not a wise man who makes
the same mistake twice.

MENANDER
(4th c. BCE, comedian)

ΩΣ ΜΕΓΑ
ΤΟ ΜΙΚΡΟΝ ΕΣΤΙΝ
ΕΝ ΚΑΙΡΩ ΔΟΘΕΝ

Great is
a small thing
given at
the right time.

MENANDER
(4th c. BCE, comedian)

ΦΙΛΟΙΣ ΕΥΤΥΧΟΥΣΙ

ΚΑΙ ΔΥΣΤΥΧΟΥΣΙΝ

Ο ΑΥΤΟΣ ΙΣΘΙ

Be the same toward your friends,
in prosperity or in hardship.

PERIANDER
(668–584 BCE, one of the Seven Sages)

ΠΑΥΡΟΙ
ΕΝ ΠοΝΩ
ΠΙΣΤΟΙ

Very few remain loyal
in times of sorrow.

PINDAR
(522–438 BCE, lyric poet)

ΤΑΣ ΝΙΚΑΣ
ΑΝΕΥ ΑΙΜΑΤΟΣ ΠΟΙΕΙΣΘΑΙ

Seek to win without bloodshed.

PITTACUS OF MYTILENE
(650–570 BCE, one of the Seven Sages)

OY TO ZHN

ΠΕΡΙ ΠΛΕΙΣΤΟΥ ΠΟΙΗΤΕΟΝ

ΑΛΛΑ ΤΟ ΕΥ ΖΗΝ

The thing to do is not to live
so as to have more,
but to lead a good life.

PLATO

(427–347 BCE, philosopher)

ΜΕΤΡΟΝ ΒΙΟΥ ΤΟ ΚΑΛΟΝ

ΟΥ ΤΟ ΤΟΥ ΧΡΟΝΟΥ ΜΗΚΟΣ

Life's worth is measured
not in its length
but in its goodness.

PLUTARCH
(47–120 CE, historian)

MHΔEN EINAI

MHTE TEχNHN ANEY MEΛETHΣ

MHTE MEΛETHN ANEY TEχNHΣ

There's no point
in ability without learning
or learning without ability.

PROTAGORAS
(c. 490 – c. 420 CE, Athenian sophist)

ΕΛΕΥΘΕΡΟΝ ΑΔΥΝΑΤΟΝ ΕΙΝΑΙ

ΤΟΝ ΠΑΘΕΣΙ ΔΟΥΛΕΥΟΝΤΑ

ΚΑΙ ΥΠΟ ΠΑΘΩΝ ΚΡΑΤΟΥΜΕΝΟΝ

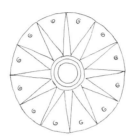

It is impossible for anybody
to be deemed free if they be a slave
to their passions and ruled by them.

PYTHAGORAS
(580–490 BCE, philosopher)

ΕΝ οΙΔΑ
οΤΙ οΥΔΕΝ οΙΔΑ

I know
one thing:
that I know
nothing.

SOCRATES
(469–399 BCE, philosopher)

ΤΩΝ ΣΩΜΑΤΩΝ ΘΗΛΥΝΟΜΕΝΩΝ

ΚΑΙ ΑΙ ΨΥΧΑΙ ΠΟΛΥ ΑΣΘΕΝΕΣΤΕΡΑΙ

ΓΙΓΝΟΝΤΑΙ

When bodies become soft,
souls weaken much also.

SOCRATES
(469–399 BCE, philosopher)

ΓΗΡΑΣΚΩ ΔΕ
ΑΕΙ ΠΟΛΛΑ ΔΙΔΑΣΚΟΜΕΝΟΣ

I grow old,
forever learning much.

SOLON

(630–560 BCE, Athenian lawmaker, one of the Seven Sages)

ΜΗΔΕΝΑ ΠΡΟ ΤΟΥ ΤΕΛΟΥΣ

ΜΑΚΑΡΙΖΕ

Consider none happy before their end.

[to King Croesus of Lydia]

SOLON
(630–560 BCE, Athenian lawmaker, one of the Seven Sages)

ΑΛΛΑ ΟΥΔΕΝ ΕΡΠΕΙ ΨΕΥΔΟΣ

ΕΙΣ ΓΗΡΑΣ ΧΡΟΝΟΥ

No falsehood can bear
the scrutiny of time.

ΔΥΣΚΟΛοΝ ΤοΝ ΕΑΥΤοΝ ΓΝΩΝΑΙ

ΕΥΚοΛοΝ ΤΩ ΑΛΛΩ ΥΠοΤΙΘΕΣΘΑΙ

It is difficult to know oneself,
but easy to counsel others.

THALES OF MILETUS
(643–548 BCE, one of the Seven Sages)

ΠΕΝΙΑ ΤΕΧΝΑΣ ΚΑΤΕΡΓΑΖΕΤΑΙ

Poverty devises skills.

THEOCRITUS
(3rd c. BCE, poet)

ΤΟΙΣ ΤΟΛΜΩΣΙΝ

Η ΤΥΧΗ ΞΥΜΦΟΡΟΣ

Fortune favours
those who dare.

THUCYDIDES
(460–394 BCE, Athenian historian)

ΝΟΜΙΖΩ ΤΟΥΣ ΑΝΘΡΩΠΟΥΣ

ΟΥΚ ΕΝ ΤΗ ΟΙΚΙΑ

ΤΟΝ ΠΛΟΥΤΟΝ

ΚΑΙ ΤΗΝ ΠΕΝΙΑΝ ΕΧΕΙΝ

ΑΛΛΑ ΕΝ ΤΑΙΣ ΨΥΧΑΙΣ

I believe it is not in their houses
that people have wealth or poverty,
but in their souls.

XENOPHON
(430–355 BCE, Athenian historian)

ΔΥΟ ΩΤΑ ΕΧΟΜΕΝ

ΣΤΟΜΑ ΔΕ ΕΝ

ΙΝΑ ΠΛΕΙΟΝΑ ΜΕΝ ΑΚΟΥΩΜΕΝ

ΗΤΤΟΝΑ ΔΕ ΛΕΓΩΜΕΝ

We have two ears
and one mouth,
to listen more
and to speak less.

ΟΥ ΓΑΡ ΤΟ ΕΙΠΕΙΝ

ΚΑΛΩΣ ΚΑΛΟΝ

ΑΛΛΑ ΤΩ ΕΙΠΟΝΤΙ

ΔΡΑΣΑΣ ΤΑ ΕΙΡΗΜΕΝΑ

What is good
is not to say good things,
but to practice
what one says.

ZENO OF CITIUM
(c. 334 – c. 262 BCE, philosopher)

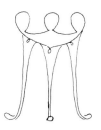

Myths Behind Words

GREEK MYTHOLOGY
IN ENGLISH WORDS AND EXPRESSIONS

Compiled by Alexander Zaphiriou
Illustrated by Panagiotis Stavropoulos

Like the constellations in the sky, words such as
'aphrodisiac', 'hubris', 'museum', 'galaxy' and 'mentor'
each contain within them a story, if only you knew to
look closely. This collection retells the myths behind
common words and expressions in English, bringing
to life the heroes, monsters and gods whose deeds
and battles have left a hidden mark on our language.

EPICTETUS

Manual
on the Art of Living

Translated by P.E. Matheson

BILINGUAL EDITION

Of all existing things, some are in our power, and
others are not in our power.' So begins the Manual or
Enchiridion of Epictetus, a collection of precepts that
together provide a powerful philosophy for daily life.
The Manual, considered to be the pinnacle of Stoic
philosophy, addresses living with integrity, self-man-
agement and personal freedom.

PYTHAGORAS

The Golden Verses

Translated by David Connolly

BILINGUAL EDITION

The essence of Pythagoras' teachings is contained in
The Golden Verses, seventy-one verses as guidelines
on how to live. Functioning as admonitions, they
link the human with the divine element and deter-
mine the point at which both elements converge to
reveal how we might ourselves attain this supreme
virtue in our everyday lives.